Options Trading For Beginners:

Options Trading Strategies Made Easy

By

Robert Alderman

ISBN-13: 978-1500414726

Table of Contents

Options Trading For Beginners: Options trading Strategies Made Easy

By Robert Alderman

First Published, 2014

Printed in the United States of America

Introduction

Options trading has gained popularity amongst the traders for the reason that the traders can merely invest small sum of money and pull it up to make greater profits quickly. Options trading is just similar to all other investments opportunities and has its specific advantages and disadvantages. With options trading in place one can as well evade their portfolio against any kind of drops in the stock market. Or it can just be the other way around that you end up becoming the "Insurance Salesperson" and start taking premium on a monthly basis. Nevertheless with so many investment opportunities that come along with Options Trading it has been found out that people lack the foundation on the working of options market. In this piece of writing we will walk you through on the basics of Options Trading and the best trading strategies that you need to implement so as to become a successful options trader.

Chapter 1. Option in the Stock Market Terminology

Option is nothing but an agreement between 2 parties to exchange something. In this agreement the holder of the option i.e. the buyer holds all the rights to sell or buy a minimum of 100 shares of any stock at a fixed preset price from the writer i.e. the options seller in stipulated period of time.

As we mentioned above that the 2 parties exchange something, wondering what are they exchanging? Yes it is the Risk that they are exchanging because Capital Markets are highly risky in nature because the stock prices keep rising and falling down and there can as well be a situation where in the capital market might crash down completely. So in order to get rid of this risk, most of the investors are willing to pay the risk premium to sellers so as to transfer the risk and the sellers are willing to accept the risk at the cost of a premium. Options Trading is done in the Options Market where the investors sell and buy call and put options.

Chapter 2. Why Opt For Options Trading?

The answer to this question is so simple, when you are trading with stocks you can merely lay a wager on up or down whereas with options in place you get 2 more additional components: the Risk Factor and the Time which let you lay a wager on the speed with which the stock will move up, how much time will the stock take to reach that level and the direction in which the stock will move. To sum it you can say that Options Trading paves way for many more options in trading.

Chapter 3. Important Terminology

Having understood that Option is nothing but a Contract, let us understand the components of the Options Contract:

1) The most common term used in the Options Trading World is the "Option Class". It implies that there are two different classes of stock options namely the put options and the call options. People who buy the options are referred to as Holders and the Sellers are known as Writers. In general the writers have a short position compared to the holders.

a) Call Option: It refers to the right of the buyer to buy predetermined quantity of a stock at a predetermined price in a given stipulated period of time.

b) Put Option: It refers to the right of the holder (buyer) to sell to sell predetermined quantity of a stock at a predetermined price in a given stipulated period of time.

2) The next most important term with regards to options trading is the "Strike Price" which denotes the price of a particular asset or stock that is to be sold or bought at the

commencement of the contract. It is the relative value between the Market value of the stock and the strike price that will help you in determining the trading value and the options premium.

3) Options Premium is found in almost all the stock options agreement and it is nothing but the amount which the option buyer has to pay to the option seller in exchange of the rights to buy or sell the options. The value of the options premium is determined by taking into consideration three most important factors the Strike Price, the Expiration Time and the unpredictability of the share.

4) Option Style is generally categorized into two types namely the "European Option Style Trading" and the "American Option Style trading". In the "European Option Style Trading" the option will get exercised only on the expiration date whereas in case of American Option Style Trading the option will get exercised till the time expires. Nowadays the American Option Style Trading is in demand over the European Style.

5) Expiration Date which has already been referred to above is another most commonly used term in Options Trading which refers to a specific time or date after which the share options will not have any more investment and financial worth. So it can be said that if a stock has passed its expiration date then it is a worthless stock. Each and every stock market has its own expiration date for their assets.

6) Underlying Asset is the actual security that the buyer is going to acquire from the seller when the option is exercised. In Option Trading terms, underlying asset can be either the shares of any of the commodities or the indices, shares of a company, any of the currencies and so on.

7) Contract Multiplier is nothing but the measure of the particular underlying asset that has to be either sold or bought all through the trading procedures.

Having understood the terminology related to the stock options it is definitely going to be helpful to you as a beginner to rule the world of options trading. It is good to have an in depth knowledge on the basic terminologies so that you can easily go ahead and do studies and research on the various tactics and strategies involved in the options trading field.

Chapter 4. Options Trading Strategies

Despite the fact that Options Trading is generally thought out to be perilous and risky, it is one of the most safest and profitable method of investment over stock trading. The best thing about Options Trading is that there are so many strategies that can be developed and each one has a different risk profile. Even though the brokerage charge with Options Trading is high when compared to any other kind of trading it can be easily balanced off as the profitability is also high when trading options. Options trading has gained popularity in spite of being highly risky because most of the traders who are driven by the greed factor have been successful in making huge profits in least time. It is possible to make huge profits provided you are managing your options with the greed motive; however losses are to be anticipated. The key mantra to becoming a successful option trader is to "be the owner of a strategy", to familiarize yourself with it confidently and implement it again and again with the use of distinct trading rules. Here are the top most Options Trading Strategies which will help you make respectable profits and minimize your risk levels:

1) Buying Call Options Strategy

This is a very straightforward and simple strategy to make the best out of the upside trend or move. This strategy is as well referred to as making a "long call trade" or the buying a call option. This is among one of the most popular and fundamental all options trading strategies. In this strategy the moment you establish a long position i.e. the moment you purchase a call option you can either:

a) Exercise your legibility to purchase the stock at its strike value either on or before the expiration.

b) Sell it.

c) Or Let it Expire.

With the Call Option strategy you just get the right to "call" it away from the owner of the stock i.e. buy the stock but definitely not the obligation to purchase the stock at the strike price of the option until its expiration date. In general the major reason to buy a call option is that, you are anticipating that the underlying option stock will see a rise up in its value much before its expiration date which is greater than the strike price plus the

13

premium that you paid to purchase the option .The only motive to buy a call option is to make the turn around so that you can sell the call at a higher value than what you paid for purchasing the option.

The maximum amount of risk that is involved with a Buy Call Option or Long Call is the sum of the primary cost of trade i.e. the premium paid and the commissions whereas the profitability is unlimited. Nevertheless since options are merely regarded as wasting assets, time is definitely going to work against you so make sure that you give yourself sufficient time to just make the right move.

2) Buying Put Options Strategy

A good investor most of the times prefer to grab profits on the down side and the best way to do so is to purchase put options. This is a simple strategy that will allow you to make profits from down move just similar to the manner in which you make profits from up move through the calls from an up move. Generally investors employ this strategy for the enclosure of stocks that they already own and if by chance they are anticipating any kind of down side in the shares.

When you buy a put option it will give you the right to put but definitely not the obligation to put it to someone else (i.e. to sell) at a specific price for a set time period i.e. the expiration date. Most of the traders think that buying put option on stocks carries less risk when compared to shorting the stock and moreover provides superior leverage and liquidity. Most of the stocks which are anticipated to be declined over time are likely to be shorted and for this reason it becomes difficult to make use of the shares particularly on a short term basis. Thus in such situations buying a put option is considered much easier as you need not borrow anything. If the stock value is in favor of you and reaches a higher value then definitely the loss is going to be unlimited as stock rallies. It has been found out that the profits when you buy a put option are hypothetically unlimited to zero mark level in case the stock value loses its ground.

3) Covered Calls Options Trading Strategy

If you are a beginner with options then definitely Covered Calls is the foremost option strategy that you should try as an investor. In general in this the investor will possess the shares of the underlying stock and is allowed to sell out of the money call for collecting the premium amount. In this strategy it is the investor who collects the premium so as to sell the call and is said to be covered by chance if the option is called away for the reason that the shares are presented to be delivered if required devoid of any add on cash outlay.

The only reason that why most of the investors implement this strategy is that they want to make extra income on the spot just before the option reaches its expiration date and becomes worthless. In such a scenario the investor is going to keep both the shares of the underlying stock and the credit accumulated and one more reason for implementing this strategy is to "lock in" some already existing profits.

The difference of the purchased stock value and the strike price of the call along with any credit that is accumulated for selling the call will give you the maximum potential profit that you can make with covered call strategy. The most profitable situation for covered call is when the stock finished right at the sold call strike. The difference between purchase value of the stock and the call premium value will give you the maximum loss in case the stock reaches a pitch all the way to 0.Nevertheless if an investor notices that the stock is rising towards the zero level then he or she will choose to close the position of the stock much before it reaches the zero level mark.

4) Cash Secured Puts Trading Strategy

This strategy generally has a sold put option which comes into existence when the strike price is less than the current stock value i.e. in out-of-the-money situation. The "Cash-Secured "part acts as a safety mesh for both the investor and the broker for the reason that there is sufficient cash that is kept on hand to purchases stocks in it is assigned.

If investors sense that there is reasonably more or less upbeat outlook for a particular stock then they will generally sell the puts and lock them with cash. This is something like instead of buying the stock out-and-out the investors sell the put and accumulate a little premium whilst waiting for the stock value to decline to a more appetizing buy in point.

In case if the investor rules out the probability of obtaining the stock then the maximum profit will be equal to the premium that is collected to sell the put and the maximum loss incurred is anyways limitless to zero which is the reason why most of the brokers allocate cash for buying the stock in case it's "put" to you. The get by for any put strategy is the strike price of the put sold minus the premium paid.

5) Option Spreads Trading Strategy

Option Spreads are an alternative in which inexperienced option trading beginners can start off with to discover this new family of imitative. The fundamental debit and credit spreads join 2 calls or 2 puts so as to gain overall debit or credit and then formulate a strategy which will provide limited risk and rewards. We can categorize Option Spreads into 4 types:

a) Bear Call Credit Spreads

b) Bull Put Credit Spreads

c) Bear Call Debit Spreads

d) Bull Put Debit Spreads

As it is implied by the name that Debit Spreads will come into existence when an investor will buy a spread by paying a debit for it and a Credit Spread will come into existence when the investor sells a spread and accumulates the credit for the same. One important thing that needs to be known here is that whether it is the debit spreads or the credit spreads the options sold or bought will be in the same expiration month and under the same underlying security.

a) Bear Call Credit Spreads

In this strategy there is a further from the money call and a sold call which is purchased. In this strategy the trader will keep the opening premium during the trading activity and after that wishes to keep a little of the credit obtained when the option is about to reach its expiration for the reason that a sold call is costlier than the purchased one. You can as well refer to this strategy of bear call credit spread as a Vertical Call Credit Spread or as a Short Call Spread.

 The rewards profile or the risk profile in this strategy is based on the money-ness of the stocks the investor chooses i.e. if they are within the money requiring a jagged downside move in the underlying stock or they are already in out of the money situation when the trade has been carried out. If you choose out of the money option then the initial amount that you have to pay is going to be smaller and thus comparatively cheaper. The reason being out-of-the-money options will not expire worthless and that is why traders agree to accepting this little amount of premium against lower risk.

The difference between strike price and premium paid will fetch you the maximum loss in case the original stock is trading higher than the long call strike. For instance if a writer is selling a call at 62.50 USD and buying a call at 65 USD by accumulating an acclaim of 90 cents in that case the upper limit for loss on his move higher than 65 USD is 1.60 USD. However if the share is trading under the short call strike value during expiration then the maximum gain will be limited to the credit collected. The get by in this case is the sum of the overall credit collected and the strike price of the purchased put.

b) Bull Put Credit Spreads

This strategy is a neutral strategy in which the trader will collect a credit and premium on opening a trade. Regardless of the fact that the spread being traded is at the money, in-the-money, or out-of-the-money, this kind of a credit spread will be willing to hold the stock at the current level. The reason being a credit will be collected when the trade activity starts and the ideal situation for this is that two of the puts should terminate valueless. For this situation to take place, the stock should be trading higher than its higher strike price during its expiration date.

This is nothing like more of an aggressive optimistic play just like the long call wherein the profits are restricted to the credit that is accumulated and as well the risk is limited to a predetermined amount regardless of whatever goes on with the original stock. The difference between the strike price and the original credit will give you the maximum loss. The get by for this is the greater strike price minus the credit.

It is obvious that as a trader you cannot collect near about 200-300% returns via Credit Spreads but it is true to the fact that you can easily make modest credits with the credit spreads strategy in place. This is best applicable in a situation where the unpredictability levels are soaring and there is possibility for the options to be sold out at an economical premium value.

c) Bull Call Debit Spreads

This strategy is reasonably bullish for people who are projecting zero downside or say reserved upside within the index, underlying stock or the ETF. In this strategy the investor will have to pay a debt for opening the spread and this 2 legged vertical spread is a combination of the same amount of purchased (long) closer to the money call and the sold (short) farther from the money calls. This among one of the traditional and conventional strategies when compared to the straight long call purchase because the sold higher strike call will be helpful in counterbalancing the risk of the bough lower strike call and the cost.

The maximum risk limit in a bull call debit spread is equal to the debit that is paid during trade along with commissions if any. As well the maximum loss in this case will be incurred if the share value is trading below the long call strike value wherein both the options are likely to expire worthless. The difference between the strike prices and the debit paid will give you the maximum potential profit. The get by in this strategy is the sum of the debit paid and the long strike and anything above that definitely the bull call spread is going to fetch you money.

d) Bear Put Debit Spreads

In this strategy the investor buy a higher strike put and at the same time sell another lower strike put by paying a debt for the whole transaction. If there is any kind of reasonable expected downside in the underlying index, ETF or stock then the investor will employ this strategy however will want to counterbalance the cost of the long put.

If the underlying stock is trading at a value greater than the long put strike during its expiration date or time then maximum loss is anticipated to be incurred which is restricted to the debit that was paid. The difference of the purchased and sold strike prices minus the premium will fetch you the expected potential profit which can be achieved if and only if the underlying stock is trading of the short put. The get by here is the difference of the strike purchased and the overall debit paid.

Having learnt about the basic options trading strategies your hand might be itching to try out the virtual options trading then definitely you must give it a try right now and choose the best broker for the same in case you have not yet.

Investors are generally of the thought that there are some special strategies, tricks and not to miss out points when it comes to Options Trading however the fact are that there are no such things involved when it comes to options as they are the most excellent investment options of the modern era. However we have some special secrets revealed here that should be employed wisely if you want to manage your risk effectively with Options Trading

Chapter 5. Nine Secrets to Option Trading Success

If you are new to the world of Option Trading then definitely you must follow the secrets mentioned here so as to become a successful option Trader:

1) Bear in mind that options are not means for gambling rather they are the most excellent risk reducing investment options available to an investor.

2) Make sure you make use of the Delta, Gamma, Theta and Vega (popularly known as the Options Greeks) to measure the level of risk.

3) Become a smart investor by managing your risk factor efficiently. Make sure that you do not posses any position that in the worst possible case can cost you more than the amount that you are anticipating to lose.

4) It generally happens that investors over trade options contracts that are inexpensive particularly when selling. Thus it is a heads up to the investors to be careful about the number of options that they are trading.

5) You should not break down in any situation so ensure that any kind of unexpected occurrence does not clear your account at any cost.

6) As an investor use your brain and invest intelligently in options rather than just expecting miracles to happen. It is suggested that you do not buy options which are far away from the money just because they are low priced, the reason being the chances of profitability with such options are negligible.

7) It is good to sell naked options rather than buying stocks because the risk involved here in is less comparatively. However just similar to stock ownership there is substantial downside risk involved with an exception. The exception here is that you can sell naked puts however if and only if you would like to purchase the shares if an exercise notice is allocated.

8) You should limit your losses in an effective manner and the best way to do so is whenever you sell an option you make sure that you buy an option too which implies that selling spreads instead of naked options.

9) Guesswork and Hope are not strategies to be implemented when it comes to options trading so whenever you feel that you are landing into a bad situation you should immediately think of reducing the risk factor. If you are simply doing nothing and expecting something good to happen in spite of knowing that you are in a bad position is just like gambling.

Conclusion

Options trading provides the investors with flexibility to invest as Options can be used with a wide range of strategies varying from traditional to high risk trading strategies whilst being customized with greater expectations rather than just stating that the stock will either go down or the stock will go up. The risk with Option Trading is also limited to the premium that you pay which makes this investment opportunity limited in risk and limitless in generating profits. Option Trading allows equivocation so the investors can defend their position against any variations in the price when the situation does not let you modify the underlying position. The best thing about option trading is that it allows the investors to gain leverage in favor a stock without committing to a trade.

Thank You Page

I want to personally thank you for reading my book. I hope you found information in this book useful and I would be very grateful if you could leave your honest review about this book. I certainly want to thank you in advance for doing this.